MR. MEN™ LITTLE MISS™ © THOIP (a SANRIO company)

Little Miss Shy goes Online Dating © 2017 THOIP (a SANRIO company)
Printed and published under licence from Price Stern Sloan, Inc., Los Angeles.
Published in Great Britain by Egmont UK Limited
The Yellow Building, 1 Nicholas Road, London W11 4AN

ISBN 978 1 4052 8869 9
66088/1
Printed in Italy

LITTLE MISS SHY
GOES ONLINE
DATING

Roger Hargreaves

Original concept and illustrations by
Roger Hargreaves

Written by
Sarah Daykin, Lizzie Daykin and Liz Bankes

EGMONT

Little Miss Shy didn't mind being single.

She had grown used to the length of her leg hair and she loved nothing more than cancelling her plans to stay in with a good book.

But there was one thing nagging at her . . .

Her mother. She liked to remind her daily that now she was in her 30s she was running out of eligible Mr Men, and eggs. And had she considered Mrs Clever's son, Mr Lawyer?

So Little Miss Shy decided it was time to find her Mr Right.

But where should she start? Her favourite place, of course. The library.

After working her way through the Romance section, she concluded that all she needed to do was go to a ball, and wait patiently until a rich brooding man whisked her off on a horse.

Little Miss Shy looked outside. 'Not many horses round here,' she thought.

Just then she noticed Mr Quiet, the librarian, looking over at her. 'He looks nice,' she thought, 'maybe I'll go and talk to him.'

But she didn't. She was too shy. And also there was a big sign saying 'KEEP QUIET' which she took very seriously.

If only she was more like her friend, Little Miss Contrary.

She didn't know if it was her PhD in Physics, or her blonde hair and orange tan, but Little Miss Contrary attracted the attention of all the men and worms in Singleland.

Little Miss Contrary couldn't wait to offer her advice. She'd been on all sorts of dates. Speed dates with Mr Rush, cheap dates with Mr Mean, expensive dates with Mr Sugardaddy, double dates, group dates, past their sell by dates . . .

'Listen babes, we need to set you up a dating profile on Mr Mendr,' she said.

'So in your profile pic you need to look sophisticated but fun, intelligent but not too intelligent, aloof yet available, effortless but also very attractive. Try pouting with a coy hand over your mouth.'

So despite the fact that she hated posing for pictures and felt a crushing pain in her chest, Little Miss Shy gave it her best shot.

. . . And this really was the best shot #nofilter.

'Now we just need to condense your personality into a few words,' said Little Miss Contrary. 'What do you like?'

'Quiet nights in, whispering and financial independence,' said Little Miss Shy.

'I'll put: being spontaneous, karaoke and having my drinks bought for me,' said Little Miss Contrary.

Little Miss Shy's first Mr Mendr match was Mr Strong.

He was a personal trainer with huge guns, great abs and a perfectly square jaw.

He suggested they go on a date to the gym and grab a protein shake. But unfortunately he got distracted by a mirror on the way and never turned up.

Mr Clumsy tried to woo her by sending pictures of himself.

He described himself as a relaxed kind of guy who liked 'hanging out' around the house.

She didn't reply.

'Oh finally, this guy looks nice . . .' whispered Little Miss Shy as she swiped through some more profiles.

His name was Mr S. Mall. His profile said he was a fun-loving guy of average height, who enjoyed basketball and reaching things on the highest shelf at the supermarket.

'Let's meet up,' said Mr S. Mall's message. 'P.S. Don't wear high heels.'

Mr S. Mall arrived to pick up Little Miss Shy for their date.

But after she opened the door and nearly trod on him, she wondered whether she could get a refund on her subscription to the dating app.

'I don't think this is going to work,' she said 'you just looked a bit taller in your profile picture.'

'But we're the perfect match!' said Mr S. Mall.

Little Miss Shy slowly backed away and shut the door.

The next day she received an invoice for the chocolates he'd brought her, his travel costs and two weeks of therapy sessions.

Little Miss Contrary had her own ideas about the perfect match for Little Miss Shy.

'Hun – I've found the future father of your children. He's single, you're single . . . you know. He's such a laugh. I don't know why no one's snapped him up, apart from the commitment phobia and the fact he lives with his mum. You are going to LOVE him!'

And Mr Funny did seem nice at first. 'Cheer up, love!' he said. 'They call me Mr Banter!'

But Mr Funny's relentless jokes were actually a bit wearing. She also couldn't really see herself with someone who wore washing up gloves in public.

'It's no use!' Little Miss Shy sobbed. 'I'll never find my Mr Right!'

And with that, she ate her microwave meal for one followed by a tub of ice-cream for eight.

Then there was a faint tap at the door.

It was Mr Quiet from the library.

He'd actually been there for six hours, but she hadn't heard him because he'd been knocking so quietly.

'Forgive me, but I was riding my horse nearby and I fell into a lake,' said Mr Quiet. 'As you can see, I'm soaked through and my manly chest is glistening with water. Might I come in and warm myself by your radiator?'

Little Miss Shy blushed like a beetroot. And put the heating on boost.

And what do you think happened next? They sat together in perfect silence. Little Miss Shy didn't know if it was something in the air or the ice-cream induced sugar rush, but she found herself asking, 'Will you be my Mr Man?'

'I'd love to,' he whispered. And then they went to bed.

That's right. He went straight home to his bed. And she got into hers.

From that day on, Little Miss Shy was able to let her leg hair grow as long as she liked and Mr Quiet was able to play World of Warcraft for six days straight, as they conducted their entire relationship from their separate homes.

And it was perfect.